Liverpool Shipbuilding

By Alan G. Jones

Many people living in the Merseyside area and beyond have heard of Cammell Laird, but how many of them are aware that shipbuilding occurred on the Liverpool side for several centuries? This is the story of the shipbuilders and the ships they built. It also includes events in these yards and their workforce who faced injury and death to build the ships that sailed the World. There are reasons that shipbuilding ended in Liverpool but carried on the opposite side of the river Mersey and it will be discussed.

The slave trade stimulated the growth in Liverpool shipbuilding. Although the building of Royal Navy ships had already started its progress.

Chapter 1

Eighteenth Century

John Okill had a yard on the south side of Salthouse Dock. In 1739 he built HMS Hastings which was the first ship built in Liverpool for the Royal Navy. His other ships for the Royal Navy were:

Aldborough 1743

Expedition 1747

Liverpool 1741

Pearl 1744

Southsea Castle 1745

Thetis 1747

Venus 1758

John Okill & Co; were the only African merchants not engaged in the slave trade. Okill died 20th August 1773 and was buried at St Peters.

Other Royal Navy ships built in Liverpool:

Adamant 1780 Baker.

Alligator 1780 Fisher

Andromeda 1784 Sutton

Anglesea 1746 Gorrill & Parks

Ariel 1781 Baker

Assistance 1781 Baker

Ceres 1781 Fearon & Webb

Daedalus 1780 Fisher

Deale Castle 1746 Golightly

Echo 1782 Barton

Furnace 1779 Fisher

Grampus 1782 Fisher

Harpy 1777 Fisher

Hyaena 1778 Fisher

Larke 1744 Golightly

Liverpool 1758 Gorill & Pownell

Looe	1745	Gorill & Parks
Nemesis	1780	Jolly & Smallshaw
Penelope	1778	Barton
Penelope	1778	Baker
Phaeton	1782	Smallshaw
Prince Henry	1747	Gorill
Racehorse	1781	Fisher
Squirrel	1785	Barton
Success	1781	Sutton.

Richard Golightly married Sarah Williamson in 1728 at St Peters when he was a shipwright. He was buried at St Nicholas on 10th September 1779.

Thomas Galley buried 28th March 1768 at St Nicholas. He was described as a boatbuilder. His Will was on 11th February 1768.

Roger Fisher died 24th March 1777. His Will was on 7th March 1777.

John Fisher died 24th May 1791 aged 51.

The first mention of a strike took place in 1777 when the frigate Hyaena was built by John Fisher's yard.

John Gorell died in 1761. His Will was on 30th May 1761. He was described as a merchant.

Peter Baker was buried February 1796 at Wavertree Holy Trinity. He was described as a merchant.

John Sutton ships:

William 1775

Andromeda 1784

Princess Royal 1782

Kent 1783

William 1796

Venerable 1798

Irlam 1800.

Richard Webb was born in 1734. He was buried at St Peter 19th July 1801 and was described as a Shipwright at Salt House Dock.

John & William Naylor Wright built several slave ships which will be mentioned later. William Naylor Wright died 13th June 1809 buried at St Nicholas church.

General Ships:

Eliza 1787

Ann 1787

Pilot boat No 2 1787

Willding 1788

Thomas 1790

Recovery 1793

Benson 1794

Beresford 1796

May 1796

John 1796

New Crescent 1796

Posthumous 1797

Earl of Liverpool 1798.

Jolly & Co;

Ship:

General Elliott 1783

John Smallshaw died 6th October 1798 age 78. In his Will 4th May 1799 he is described as a shipbuilder of Liverpool.

Ship:

Duke of Athol 1794.

Dwerryhouse

Ships:

Gascoyne 1791

Ann Philippa 1792.

Edward Grayson founded a firm in 1740. In 1759 his son also called Edward was baptized at St Peter. Edward senior died 1st April 1785. His son built the following ships.

Young Ralph 1798

Marquis of Kildare ...

The Watt 1797.

Slave ships built in Liverpool.

Adventure	1802
Aeolus	1787
Aggie	1777
Agreeable	1786
Albion	1783
Amacree	1788
Argyle	1807
Badger	1775
Beaver	1796
Bell	1788
Betsey	1768
Betsey	1790
Bloom	1789
Bolton	1792
Bootle	1805
Brooks	1781
Chambers	1794
Echo	1791
Elizabeth	1806
Elliott	1783
Enterprize	1790
Falmouth	1806
Fly	1772
Goodrich	1799

Hannah	1786	
Hannah	1795	
Hannah	1797	
Harriot	1786	
Iris	1783	
Jane	1805	
John Bull	1799	Wright (shipbuilder)
Little Joe	1784	
Liver	1786	
Lord Nelson	1798	
Lottery	1796	
Martha	1788	
Mary	1806	
Mary Ann	1807	
Molly	1769	
Molly	1778	
Mosley Hill	1782	
Nelly	1798	
Nicholson	1778	
Nicholson	1802	
Orange Grove	1790	
Othello	1781	
Othello	1786	
Otter	1797	

Paragon	1800	
Parr	1797	Wright
Plover	1788	
Ponsonby	1796	Wright
Princess Amelia	1798	
Princess Royal	1783	
Princess Royal	1790	
Ranger	1789	
Rose	1806	
Saint Ann	1797	
Sally	1782	
Sarah	1797	Wright
Sarah	1803	
Tarleton	1789	
Tarleton	1796	
Tiger	1800	
True Briton	1775	
Union	1791	
Union	1805	
Vanguard	1799	
Will	1797	
William Heathcote	1800	Wright
Young Hero	1785	

The slave trade was a triangular trade going first to Africa they took manufactured goods mostly and traded them for slaves and bound them tightly in the ships. They were treated badly and were transported mainly to the West Indies. The ships brought back raw materials such as sugar for the home market.

Chapter 2

Nineteenth Century

Edward Grayson shipbuilder fought a duel with William Sparling of the 10th Regiment of Dragoons. Grayson was killed on 26th February 1804. He was buried on 7th March 1804 at St Thomas.

The duel arose from an anonymous letter received by Sparling (who was at the time engaged to Anne Renshaw) the letter reflected on the character of the young lady's family. Her father was Rev. Samuel Renshaw (who lived in Bold Street.)

William Sparling gave himself up and was tried at Lancaster Assizes on 4th April 1804. He was acquitted.

At the village of Hale in the church of St Mary's is the grave of James Rathbone it states 'To the Memory of James Rathbone of Liverpool shipbuilder who departed this life May 13th 1826 aged 69. His illness was borne with Christian fortitude and resignation. His character as a Husband and father and truly honest man.'

Rathbone's grave is situated near the one of John Middleton (1578-1623) the so called 'Childe of Hale' who stood supposedly 9 feet 3 inches tall.

James Rathbone in 1821 lived at 99 St James Street. He was in business with Henry Leathom. The shipbuilders' yard was at 14 Trentham street.

Satellite was a ship built by Rathbone in 1826.

Peter Chaloner was a shipbuilder in Liverpool from 1805. He married Dorothea Summers in the same year at St Paul. He was described as a merchant. His Will was in 1857 and it stated he was a merchant shipbuilder. Thomas Chaloner was a shipbuilder in 1851 born in Liverpool. Vincent Chaloner in 1861 was described as a merchant and insurance agent. He is mentioned as a shipbuilder.

Ships built by Chaloner.

Fiery Cross 1860

Knight Templar 1861

Monarchy 1851

Oncle Felix 1859

Samson 1846

West Derby 1855

Robert Clarke began as a shipbuilder in c1815. In 1841 he was a shipbuilder.

Ships

George Rainy 1861

Marian 1847

Liverpool 1852

Niphon 1860

Sir Henry Havelock 1862

Royden began as a shipbuilder in c1810. Thomas Royden

was born in Woodchurch, Cheshire c1792. On 17th May 1831 Thomas Bland Royden son of Thomas and Nancy shipbuilder was baptized at Toxteth St James. Their yard was at 5 Baffin Street. Thomas senior of Frankby Hall was buried at Frankby 19th September 1868 aged 76. The Liverpool Echo 11th April 1893 reported 'An Old Liverpool Shipbuilding Firm. Retirement of Mr T.B.Royden.'

Ships

Albanian 1870

Andean 1872

Anne Royden 1856

Annie Worrall 1851

Auk 1871

Bahiana 1872

Batanga 1871

Beatrice 1864

Bernard 1870

British Admiral 1873

British Consul 1866

British Envoy 1866

British General 1874

British king 1869

British Sceptre 1868

British Statesman 1867

Cabenda 1872

Canadian 1872

Casablanca 1868

Ceara 1861

Chilena 1854

Claribel 1872

Deva 1873

Eaton Hall 1870

Eboe 1870

Elmina 1873

Ethiopia 1873

Finisterre 1873

Frankby 1857

Glencorse 1868

Glenesk 1869

Glengarry 1873

Golden Gate 1869

Haddon Hall 1868

Huacho 1870

Inca 1862

Iquique 1871

Ismyr 1850

Ismyr 1868

Knight Companion 1865

La Zingara 1860

Lady Bird 1866

Lady Lawrence 1868

Ligurian 1874

Lisbon 1874

Lisbonense 1871

Locksley Hall 1869

Lord Canning 1867

Lord Strathnairn 1867

M.C Nelson 1868

Malleney 1868

Mersey 1852

Monrovia 1863

Our Queen 1860

Pendragon 1868

Rallus 1870

Romeo 1869

Roscote 1863

Saint Magnus 1867

Saint Marnock 1867

Saint Monan 1868

San Luis 1864

Sarah Anderson 1865

Savoir Faire 1863

Sir Henry Lawrence 1865

Soudan 1870

Springwood 1862

The Douglas 1869

Vespasian 1872

Viola 1868

Zadne 1869

Zena 1871.

Joseph Steel began as a shipbuilder c1834. He was born c1821.In 1851 he was described as a shipbuilder. By 1861 he was a shipowner and in 1871 he was a merchant.

Ship:

Lohengrin 1874

Matthew Clover began as a shipbuilder c1825. He was born in 1795 from Gateshead. He passed away in 1845. The firm was taken over by other members of the family. They eventually moved their business to the Birkenhead side.

Ship

Bengal 1868

By the 1830s Canada's shipbuilders were competing successfully with Liverpool shipbuilders because they had unlimited supplies of cheap timber and paid lower wages than Liverpool shipbuilders. By 1854 nearly 50 per cent of Liverpool fleet had been built in Canada.

Michael Humble was born in Liverpool in 1795. In 1851 he was described as a master shipwright. He went into business with Thomas Milcrest who was born c1796. He moved to Hastings, Sussex and died in 1855. Humble moved to Wales living at Gwersyllt Park. He became a magistrate. He died in 1870.

James Hodgson's shipbuilding yard was in Toxteth Dock

Ship:

Britannia 1847

William Seddon was born c1785 in Appleton, Cheshire.

Ships:

Chamcook 1839

Steadfast 1839

Queen 1839

Fortfield ...

Henry Jordan was born in Liverpool in c1801. He later joined with Tucker their shipyard was at Baffin Street. In 1849-1851 the firm was Jordan and Findlay.

Ship

Excelsior ...

In 1853 the firm was Jordan and Getty, two years later it was Getty, Jones and Company while in 1857-58 Josiah Jones junior, conducted the firm on his own. He was born in Liverpool c1835. In 1860 it became Jones, Quiggin and Company. The firm it is believed to have been the first to have used steel in the construction of ships in Liverpool. Five years later they formed the Liverpool Shipbuilding Company with a capital of £300,000. They ended about 1880.

Quiggin built ship:

Southern

Liverpool Shipbuilding company ships:

Ararat 1871

Borwick Rails 1871

British Navy 1869

Broughty Castle 1870

Fgypt 1871

Maypocho 1869.

Peter Cato (1802-1875) in 1851 he was living at Rodney Street. He was born in Whitby, Yorkshire.

Ships:

Compage 1864

David Harrison 1853

Lota 1861

Peruana 1850

Salvadorena 1855

Tarapaca 1862

Tiger 1853

John Dawson was born c1799 in Lancaster. In 1851 he was employing 42 men. His shipbuilding yard was in Duke's Dock. By 1871 he was still a shipbuilder.

Ships:

Caboceer 1863

Dreadnought 1859

Harvest Home 1866

Twin Brothers 1865

A Sample of Liverpool built Ships

Abbey 1838

Abbots Read 1838

Agnes 1834

Albanian 1838

Alecto 1825

Alice 1835

Alice Jane 1836

Allerton 1822

Amelia 1826

Ann 1847

Ann Lockerby 1834

Ann Powell 1847

Ann & Ellen 1839

Anna Dixon 1842

Anne Baldwin 1831

Anne Jane 1838

Antelope 1845

Appleton 1833

Arab 1825

Arabia 1825

Ardencraig 1848

Argentina 1834

Arica 1831

Aura 1812

Bahamian 1826

Balkan 1849

Bangalore 1841

Barbadian 1832

Barkhill 1845

Beethoven 1841

Bellairs 1845

Betsey Hall 1833

Bland 1829

Bolton 1822

Bootle 1820

Bounty Hall 1816

Brazilian 1824

Brazilian 1841

Buenos Arrin 1840

Castries 1836

Centaur 1839

Charles Hamerton 1833

Charlotte 1844

Chatham 1827

Cheshire 1831

Chimborazo 1841

Cicely 1828

Commerce 1825

Commerce 1833

Competitor 1839

Corinthian 1840

Countess of Sefton 1847

Creamore 1839

Creole 1839

Cuba 1824

Currency 1839

Denison 1831

Devon 1840

Diana 1847

Dickey Sam 1841

Dorisana 1843

Duke of Athol 1794

Duke of Wellington 1842

Dyson 1826

Earl of Powis 1836

Edward Boustead 1842

Eliza Johnston 1834

Eliza Sanders 1834

Elizabeth 1818

Elizabeth Wood 1839

Ellen Jenkinson 1823

Emma 1833

Emma Graham 1838

Emperor 1843

Empress 1847

Endymion 1847

Equator 1845

Euphrates 1834

Fanny Chapman 1850

Favourite 1785

Favourite 1845

Frances 1832

Frances 1821

Gem 1844

George 1848

Georgina 1846

Geraldine 1850

Governor 1840

Gratitude 1830

Hannah Salkeld 1845

Hardware 1821

Harriet Humble 1845

Helena 1838

Henrietta 1838

Henrietta 1833

Hermes 1836

Higginson 1814

Hope 1801

Huddersfield 1825

Irlam 1836

Iron Prince 1844

Isabella 1835

Isabella 1821

Isabella 1824

Isadora 1835

Jaeger 1848

Jamaica 1837

Jamaica 1834

Jane 1846

John Begg 1820

John Brooks 1831

John Bull 1838

John Heys 1820

John Laird 1842

John Macvivar 1841

John O'Gaunt 1835

John Ormerod 1826

John Johnstone 1832

Joseph Yeo 1840

Joshua Waddington 1844

Judith 1829

Lady Florence 1812

Lady Rowena 1827

Lahore 1845

Lalla 1843

Lancashire Witch 1835

Lancaster 1838

Lancastrian 1849

Laura 1829

Lima 1845

Liver 1822

Livingstone 1840

Loodianah 1846

Luna 1819

Lydia 1841

Maia 1839

Malibran 1843

Margaret 1848

Margaret Ridley 1849

Maria 1812

Maria & Fanny 1839

Marshal Bennett 1820

Mary Ann Webb 1832

Mary Ann Bibby 1825

Mary Ellen 1839

Mary Ellen 1839

Mary Hannah 1844

Mary Hartley 1836

Mary Imrie 1838

Mary Marsden 1838

Mary Somerville 1835

Mary Woods 1846

May 1848

Meg of Meldon 1840

Mersey 1824

Mexican Packet 1840

Murray 1824

Mysore 1840

Naomi 1848

Nestor 1825

Oak 1836

Orford 1812

Orixa 1836

Otterspool 1834

Panic 1848

Panope 1841

Paragon 1837

Parker 1830

Pilgrim 1839

Polly 1785

Posthumous 1798

Principe Alberto 1840

Priscilla 1838

Providence 1839

Rachel 1826

Rance 1849

Ranger 1834

Rapid 1822

Richard 1845

Richard 1826

Richard Brown 1844

Ripley 1827

Robert Finnie 1829

Robert Whiteway 1839

Rock 1837

Roseanna 1840

Royal Saxon 1829

Saint Vincent 1840

Samson 1846

Sandbach 1828

Shaw 1801

Sir John Berres 1830

Sphynx 1839

Success 1841

Swithamley 1844

Syria 1841

Tagus 1841

Tapley 1833

The Duke 1843

Theodosia 1830

Thomas Dempsey 1823

Thomas Worthington 1833

Tom Banks 1839

Urgent 1840

Velore 1842

Viscount Sandon 1842

Wannan 1840

Warwick 1825

William Fisher 1844

William Jardine 1836

Wilsons 1823

Winifred 1842

Woodstock 1837

Steam Ships

Flecha 1846

Hibernia 1847

McAdam 1836

Newcastle 1834

Troubador 1841

Iron Ships

Emma 1847

Hibernia 1847

Troubador ...

Sailing Vessels.

Richard Cobden 1844.

In 1851 Thomas Wilson was described as a shipbuilder living in Much Woolton. He was born in Liverpool c1807. By 1881 he was retired living in Spital, Cheshire now in Wirral. He died 7th November 1885 in Llandudno, Wales.

Ships:

United States 1840

Hindostan 1842

Duke of Cornwall 1842

Bentinck 1843

Albert 1845

Duke of Lancaster 1846.

Thomas Vernon was born in Davenham, Cheshire c1799. In 1861 he was staying at a hotel called Childwall Abbey. He died 7th September 1861 at the residence of William Heatly Esquire High Hatton Hall in Shropshire. A few years ago I made a visit to

Shropshire to see the Hall. It was quite isolated and in beautiful countryside. The Hall was a magnificent building.

John Vernon took over control of the company after the death of his father. He employed 70 men and 20 boys. He died in 1874.

Ships:

Achilles 1866

Astronomer 1859

Bayard 1864

Beann-vamha 1861

Brackley 1859

Bridgewater 1857

Camana 1865

Chevey Chase 1863

Childwall Abbey 1863

Cicero 1861

Cognac 1860

Cordillera 1866

Cormorant 1865

Cornwallis 1862

Duleep Singh 1863

Enniskillen 1854

Esmeralda 1866

Flechero 1866

Glenlora 1864

Heather Bell 1865

Hertfordshire 1863

Kenyon 1862

Llanddulas 1857

Lord Lyndhurst 1861

Macedonia 1867

Mount Vernon 1863

Naturalist 1863

Oriente 1866

Pasithea 1862

Philip Nelson 1864

Preussischer Adler 1845

Prince Arthur 1864

Prince Patrick 1856

Rajpoot 1864

Rimac 1865

Robert Lees 1863

Rokeby Hall 1863

Sabrina 1844

Santa Rosa 1862

Sarah & Emma 1860

Slieve Donard 1859

Sword Fish 1864

Talisman 1864

Tamaya 1862

Tomas 1865

Troubadour 1856

Valparaiso 1866

Vernon 1864

Vigil 1862

Warwickshire 1862

Advance 1855.

William B Jones was born c1800. He was born in Liverpool. His yard was at 15 Walter Street.

George W Jones was born in Liverpool in c1838 and was a Boilermaker and Iron shipbuilder.

Ships built by Jones

Aconcagua 1859

Aminta 1862

Derbyshire 1863

Despatch 1856

Evelyn 1863

Helen Scott 1863

Hercules 1846

San Lorenzo 1861

Seaforth 1862

Staffordshire 1862

Victoria Cross 1863

Water Lily 1862.

William Cowley Miller was baptized 22nd April 1803 at Charles the Martyr church in Plymouth, Devon son of Robert Miller & Catherine. In Liverpool in 1851 he employed 104 men in his shipbuilding yard which was in Brunswick Dock.

The Liverpool Mercury Tuesday 17th January 1865 reported 'Foundering of the Steamer: Loss of Leia. Upward of Forty Lives Lost. Mr Thomas Miller was the son of our respected townsman Mr W C. Miller one of the municipal representatives of South Toxteth Ward. The deceased was a young man of great promise and has been for several years an active partner in the firm originated by his father, that of W.C.Miller and sons, the extensive shipbuilder of this town. He was about 27 years of age, married and leaves a widow and two children. It appears he intended to proceed in the vessel as far as Holyhead, his object being, as is customary with shipbuilders, to ascertain the working of the vessel and her sea-going capacities.'

Ships:

Arcquipa 1862

Arica 1862

Atahualpa 1865

Emily Waters 1861

Enrique 1870

Helen 1860

Helen 1869

Saint Winifred 1870

Steady 1860

Wyre 1862.

Hugh Molleneux Lawrence was born in 1832 in Liverpool. In 1861 he was a master engineer employing 83 men and 15 boys. His yards where at Sandon Engine Works 25 Boundary Street and Sefton Street. In 1871 he was living on his own means in Chorlton Upon Medlock. In 1891 he had his own means, but was living in North Meols, Lancashire. In 1901 he was a retired engineer living in Whalley Range. He died in 1902.

Ships:

Bianca 1862

Halton Castle 1862

Iron Duke 1863

May Flower 1862

Monmouthshire 1863.

In 1861 Thomas Hunter Holderness was 43 years old and born in Hull. He was described as a shipowner. His yard was at 16 Sefton Street, Toxteth Park.

Ships:

Duke of Edinburgh 1867

Eliza Walker 1865

Ta Lee 1864

Zeminder 1864.

In 1871 Richard B Hooper was born c1834 in Hamburg, but a British subject. He was living, at the time, in Bootle and described as a shipwright employing 19 men and 16 boys.

Ships:

Alert 1870

Louise 1871.

William Sims in 1861 was born c1819 in Sunderland. He was described as a master shipwright. His yard was South Side Duke's Dock.

Ship:

Alice Holden 1863

John Thompson's yard was at Herculaneum Dock

Ship:

Sea Swallow.

John Stretch Hart was born in Pendleton, Lancashire in c1835

Ships:

Briarley 1862

Coldinghame 1866

Oriflamme 1865

Rajah 1864

Ranee 1864.

Alderman James Jack died 26th April 1880 the flag was at half mast at the Town Hall.

He was a native of Scotland.

In 1840 he worked as a night foreman for Thomas Vernon and Company, iron shipbuilders.

He commenced business in a humble way in Dublin Street.

In 1871 James Jack was an engineer and shipbuilder. His yard was at Victoria Engine Works, Boundary Street West.

He eventually attained a position which gave him a well earned reputation it was subsequently increased when David Rollo, a fellow Scot who was born c1821, joined the large and growing concern.

Jack had been ill for some months so he went to stay at a Southport hotel for the benefit of his health. He had a fit of paralysis and became semi-unconscious and eventually died.

He was a strong Conservative, but was described as a kind and considerate employer, a true friend and although without any attainments he attempted to do the best of his abilities.

Ship:

Venezuelan 1865

William Hodgson Potter was born in Hull in 1826. His shipbuilding was at Queen's Dock. He died in 1904 at his residence Cloverley in Brimstage which was then in Cheshire present day Wirral. He was buried at All Saints church Thornton Hough.

Ships:

Allahabad 1864

Bedfordshire 1863

Borrowdale 1868

British Ambassador 1873

Casma 1869

Charles Batters 1873

Chasca 1869

Chrysomerie 1873

Ennerdale 1874

Iron Queen 1863

Kalahome 1867

Lady Darling 1864

Liffey 1870

Macedon 1870

Navarre 1866

Siam 1865

Thomas Stephens 1869

Wanderer 1891.

Robert Evans was born in c1811 in Liverpool. In 1861 he was a master shipbuilder employing 1140 men and 85 boys. In 1891 John Evans was born in c1843 in Liverpool. Evans shipyard was at Brunswick Dock. John died in 1910.

Ships:

Adelaide Mary ...

Angola 1870

Archibald Fuller 1868

Barracouta 1864

Bella 1863

Birkenhead 1872

Cardigan Castle 1870

Carnarvon Castle ...

Caroca 1864

Castlehead 1869

Cincora 1874

Clevedon 1868

Coronilla 1865

County of Anglesea 1877

Crocus 1873

Dagny 1889

Dahlia 1872

Don Guillermo 1866

Explorer 1866

Finzel 1861

Frankfurt Hall 1869

Frieda 1870

Garland 1865

Gladbrook 1877

Hawarden Castle 1869

Itata 1873

Itata 1883

Knowsley Hall 1873

Lalla Rookh 1876

Linda 1873

Lord Clive 1871

Lynton 1894

Meinwen 1892

Metopolis 1887

Miniera 1882

Mistley Hall 1874

Montgomery Castle 1869

Rimac 1872

Rydal Hall 1874

Sandviken 1871

Santa Lucia 1866

Seatoller 1866

Sylhet 1866

Tenby Castle 1868

Theophane 1868.

John Jones & sons in 1858 were engineers, boilermakers & millwrights their yard was at 33 Williams street, Great Howard

Street. By 1898 the company were shipbuilders at Brunswick Dock. The founder of the company was John Jones born c1802 in Denbighshire, Wales. His sons Charles Jones was born c1840 who in 1891 was a master engineer and shipbuilder another son was James Jones born c1842. In 1881 James was a town councillor. The Liverpool echo 4th February 1884 reported his horrific death 'Shocking Death Of A Birkenhead Alderman: On Saturday evening a shocking accident took place at Ainsdale Station on the Southport Railway, whereby Mr James Jones, an alderman of Birkenhead, lost his life. It appears that Mr Jones, accompanied by one of his sons and a friend had been on Saturday on a visit to Sandringham Farm, Ainsdale of which he is the tenant. After leaving the farm to return to Liverpool by the train due at Ainsdale Station at 5.50 they had to cross the metals to reach the platform. Mr Jones was walking a little behind his son and the other gentleman, and from some as yet unexplained cause he did not appear to have observed the near approach of the train. At all events he appears in attempting to get over the line to have stopped right in front of the engine with the result that he was caught by one of the buffers and buried with considerable violence between the metals, the blow carrying him forward five or six yards. Though the train was moving slowly at the time, the unfortunate gentleman's position does not seem to have been discovered until nearly the whole of the carriages had passed over him. When it was brought to a standstill the greatest excitement took place regarding the sad calamity, and much anxiety was manifested by those who were on the platform waiting the arrival of the train and those who occupied the carriages. The first thought of everyone was directed towards the best means of extricating the mutilated body of Mr Jones from underneath the rear portion of the train, but in the gathering darkness of the evening this was a task of some difficulty. It was first seen that his limbs were free of the rails, and then the train was very slowly drawn forwards clear of the body. It was seen that Mr Jones was unconscious, though not dead and that in addition to the wheels having passed over both legs he had sustained a serious wound in the head. He was gently lifted from his position, and at the request of his son, who was almost overwhelmed with grief, was placed in the guard's van of the train, to be taken to Liverpool. Dr Glazebrook, of Liverpool, who happened to be a passenger in the train and who exerted himself along with others to try and alleviate the sufferings of Mr Jones rode in the van with him. Mr Jones, however, did not regain consciousness, and died within twenty minutes of the accident, and before the train reached Bootle Station. On arriving at Liverpool, the body was taken from the train to the Northern Hospital ambulance waggon, which had been telegraphed for, in the hope that something might be done to save Mr Jones's life. Mr F. Johnston, one of the house surgeons at the hospital, along with Dr McLaren, received the body in the ambulance waggon at Exchange Station.

This morning the flags were at half-mast on several public buildings in Birkenhead, and at Woodside Ferry, out of respect to the memory of the deceased.'

Ships:

Aphrodita 1858

Tiger 1867.

In 1891 Caleb Smith was described as a shipbuilder. He was born in c1848 in Liverpool. His shipbuilding took place at Toxteth Dock.

The end for Liverpool shipbuilding was reported in the Liverpool Mercury dated 29th July 1899 it stated 'Although shipbuilding on the Lancashire side of the Mersey has practically become a matter of the past, the tapping on the head of the last nail in the coffin of the once considerable industry comes as a very unpleasant knell…as the extension scheme of the Dock Board made that imperative...Now a time is fixed for a total annilation of a trade which earned for Liverpool shipbuilders the highest...in every port in the World for the Mersey-built ships hoisted their flags in every corner of the globe...Three remaining yards John Jones & Co; Messrs Evans and sons and Messrs Caleb Smith...the ground they now occupy will be employed giving that accommodation to the shipping port which is so urgently needed, owing to the development of the trade of Liverpool.'

Chapter 3

Incidents of problems in Liverpool Shipbuilding yards.

Working in shipbuilding yards could be dangerous places as these two incidents reveal. Liverpool Echo 4th November 1887 states 'James Gillmore forty-five years of age residing at Lower Harrington Street who is a labourer employed by Messrs T.B.Royden & Co; shipbuilders, Liverpool was working on a vessel...at the yard...Queen's Dock...when he...fell into the hold and fractured his skull.'

Liverpool Mercury 10th February 1891 stated 'Fatal Accident At A Liverpool Shipbuilding Yard...David Parsons aged 50...was in the employ of Messrs T.B.Royden...the deceased a driller was working on a new vessel and fell into the chamber of the vessel.'

Shipbuilding yards could be dangerous for the shipbuilders as these two incidents reveal. In 1862 a fire took place at the yard of

Cato, Miller and Co; Brunswick Dock. It caused damage worth £1,200.

The Liverpool Mercury 7th December 1864 stated 'Last night, about twelve o'clock, a fearful fire broke out in the yard of W and H Potter and Co; shipbuilders of Blackstone Street, at the back of the Queen's Dock, will perhaps, before it is extinguished prove to be of the most extensive that has of late taken place in Liverpool. We understand it broke out in the yard, its course caught the timber in the a joining yard Messrs Hart and Sinnet of Baffin Street. A great quantity of timber and the frame of a vessel were burnt, as well as a block of workshops. A great part of the machinery in Messrs Potter's yard has been totally destroyed...'

Finally, we have come to the end of this book on Liverpool Shipbuilding their end came in 1899 this work has contained the shipbuilders' biographies and some of the ships they built. Both they and their workforce took risks. When their end came Liverpool was to develop more as a port, but arguably it always had been and even today the port and shipbuilding carry on and on...

THE END...

www.ingramcontent.com/pod-product-compliance
Lightning Source LLC
LaVergne TN
LVHW052109160826
845678LV00015B/3445